THE THRIVING WORKPLACE SERIES

VOLUME 2

LEADING CHANGE

The 5 Tensions to Manage
for Successful Transformation

TIM ARNOLD

Leaders for Leaders Inc.
2866 Prince William Street
PO Box 25
Jordan Station, ON, L0R 1S0
(289) 723 2546

Ordering Information:
Special discounts are available on quantity purchases by corporations, associations, and others. For details, contact the publisher at the address or phone number above.

www.LeadersForLeaders.ca

CONTENTS

THE THRIVING WORKPLACE SERIES

You want to be a great leader. Someone who makes a positive difference through the work you do *and* in the lives of the people you do it with. A person who inspires others through your positivity and passion. The kind of leader everyone wants to work for.

In order to do this, you need to be successful at three things:

1. Building effective teams,

2. Leading people through change, and

3. Fostering a healthy workplace culture.

The problem is most organizations are broken, which forces you to spend too much of your time wrestling with conflicting values and refereeing unhealthy friction. This can leave you feeling discouraged and unsupported.

It shouldn't be this hard! You deserve a trusted roadmap to help you build the thriving workplace you know is possible. The Thriving Workplace Series is that roadmap.

Through my experience owning a for-profit business, launching a social enterprise, and directing a homeless shelter, I understand how hard it is to lead in challenging situations. This is why I'm driven to help leaders just like you navigate the road to success.

In working with incredible leaders ranging from Nobel Peace Prize winners to Fortune 500 CEOs, I've learned that the secret to success is to embrace the very thing most people avoid: tension. Great leaders find *healthy* tension in the following key areas:

Next-Level Teamwork
(Volume 1 of The Thriving Workplace Series)

1. Focusing on Tasks AND Relationships
2. Leveraging Structure AND Flexibility
3. Communicating Truthfully AND Tactfully
4. Promoting Collaboration AND Independence
5. Increasing Empowerment AND Accountability

Leading Change
(Volume 2 of The Thriving Workplace Series)

1. Embracing Innovation AND Consistency
2. Validating Facts AND Feelings
3. Focusing on the Short Term AND the Long Term
4. Promoting Planning AND Action
5. Valuing Complexity AND Simplicity

Winning Culture
(Volume 3 of The Thriving Workplace Series)

1. Focusing on People AND Results
2. Respecting Rules AND Risk

3. Fostering Critical Analysis AND Encouragement

4. Promoting Decentralized Freedom AND Centralized Coordination

5. Valuing Work AND Home

Too many people spend most of their waking hours working for unhealthy organizations and in dysfunctional teams. Sadly, one of the main reasons for this is ineffective leaders who don't have the skills or courage to face tension head-on. But not you!

The purpose of this playbook series is to help you tap into the power of healthy tension so that you can unleash your true leadership potential and help your organization thrive.

By putting the concepts and principles of these playbooks into action, you will make your leadership stand out from the crowd. You will be responsible for creating an environment where everyone loves their work, who they get to do it with, and the impact it's having.

Let's do this!

LEADING CHANGE

The 5 Unavoidable Tensions

1. Embracing Innovation AND Consistency
2. Validating Facts AND Feelings
3. Focusing on the Short Term AND the Long Term
4. Promoting Planning AND Action
5. Valuing Complexity AND Simplicity

To thank you for purchasing this playbook, I want to provide you with a free resource that will allow you to create a personal action plan around key concepts and big ideas.

Simply visit www.timarnold.ca/change to download the Personal Action Plan. This digital journal includes chapter summaries, tension maps, and assessment grids as well as space for you to create a plan you can immediately put into action.

WWW.TIMARNOLD.CA/CHANGE

CHAPTER 1

(MIS)MANAGING CHANGE

Why Most Change Initiatives
Underdeliver and Divide

O ver the past month, I've worked with three different clients, each committed to implementing meaningful change:
a Fortune 500 company rolling out a sophisticated CRM system to
boost efficiency and client service, a dedicated fire chief updating
equipment to enhance safety and agility, and a school board pio-
neering inclusive programs for every child's sense of belonging.
The intent of the change is universally positive, yet, in each case,
leaders are navigating through a sea of resistance, unintended
and costly mistakes, and escalating team conflict.

Can you relate to this struggle? If you're steering through
change that isn't delivering the outcomes you anticipated, you're
not alone.

Interestingly, despite the diversity of my clients, when I hear
about the challenges they're dealing with during change, a pat-
tern emerges, almost as if there's a universal cast of characters
at play in every team. It appears that, regardless of the setting,

teams navigating change will typically include all of the following individuals:

1. **Disgruntled Dana** – Dana is deeply set in the old ways and goes out of her way to vocalize her discontent. Dana often remarks, "Why fix what isn't broken?," and is quick to highlight any hiccup in the new processes.

2. **Resistant Raj** – He's not necessarily angry, but Raj is firmly rooted in past methods and fails to get with the program, often joking about being too much of an "old dog" to adopt "new tricks."

3. **Confused Chris** – Chris genuinely wants to embrace change but finds himself lost in the transition, leading to heightened stress, self-doubt, and recently, an increase in absenteeism as he struggles to get his head around the new direction.

4. **Trailblazing Terry** – Ambitious and eager for recognition, Terry is overzealous in demonstrating his agreement and alignment with the new changes, alienating himself from colleagues who find his enthusiasm excessive and annoying.

5. **Utopian Uma** – As the leader of the team, Uma is constantly pointing out how broken the current reality is and how this change will be the solution to everyone's problems. However, her idealism seems detached from on-the-ground realities, causing a rift in trust as her team yearns for more practical and empathetic leadership.

Do these characters sound familiar? Have you encountered them in your workplace? It's intriguing, isn't it, how change often reveals our less-admirable traits and creates division rather than unity. Why does change seem to be a catalyst for conflict rather than a catalyst for cooperation as it should be?

If you find yourself asking that question, it's not just you. In my weekly interactions with professionals from various sectors, I've witnessed the profound impact that ineffective change management can have—not just on team morale but on organizational performance.

But it doesn't have to be this way!

Over the last two decades, I've facilitated transformation for countless organizations—from the hallways of the United Nations, to the boardrooms of Fortune 500 companies, to the conference rooms of community-centred non-profits. I've seen firsthand that with the right approach, it's possible to pivot from outdated processes to dynamic, high-performing ones without the team falling apart along the way. Change management doesn't have to be a tale of unfulfilled promises and division—it can be a story of unity and progress.

However, there's a catch.

To lead change effectively, you must possess the courage and skill to confront what many leaders avoid—tension. That's right, the key to next-level change management is embracing tension rather than running from it.

Tension is the force that allows you to hold two opposing ideas in your mind at the same time. On the surface, the ideas appear to be conflicting, but when you look beneath the surface, you find that one side simply can't exist in a healthy way without the other. It's not about choosing between two options but about finding dynamic balance between them. It's about shifting from Either/Or thinking to Both/And thinking.

In fact, according to bestselling authors Chip and Dan Heath, "any time you're tempted to think, 'Should I do this OR that?,' instead, ask yourself, 'Is there a way I can do this AND that?'"[1]

Every day, we naturally balance the rhythm of inhaling *and* exhaling over 20,000 times. For well-being, we need to embrace both activity *and* rest. In relationships, we need to take care of others *and* take care of ourselves. Parenthood calls for both structure *and* flexibility. In our teams, we need to be both task-driven *and* relationship-focused. As a business owner, I need to pursue profit *and* purpose.

The encouraging reality is that, as illustrated by these examples, you've been navigating tensions all your life. You can see how trying to eliminate tension by picking one side is as absurd as choosing only to inhale all day—you'd soon be gasping for air.

This principle is crucial when managing change. Tension is inevitable during a change, and if you favour one side to the neglect of the other, your change is bound to fail. But by managing tension effectively, you allow your team and organization to get unstuck and leverage change as a competitive advantage.

When delving into the world of change management, we discover a landscape full of paradoxical tensions, but I've realized that, basically, they all boil down to five:

1. Embracing Innovation AND Consistency

2. Validating Facts AND Feelings

3. Focusing on the Short Term AND the Long Term

4. Promoting Planning AND Action

5. Valuing Complexity AND Simplicity

The core of successful change management lies in understanding and leveraging these five unavoidable tensions.

CHANGE REIMAGINED

The data is discouraging: Nearly 70% of change initiatives in organizations fail to meet their goals.[2] It's not that the changes are wholly unsuccessful, but they often fall short of the transformative impact they aim for.

This phenomenon isn't confined to the corporate world either; personal resolutions often falter in a similar way. Whether it's committing to regular exercise, reducing screen time, or improving our eating habits, too frequently, our best intentions dissolve into a cycle of disappointment and frustration. Change management, as commonly practiced, tends to underwhelm and disillusion.

The strategies outlined in this book are designed to flip the script. By understanding and applying the practical "plays" outlined in the following pages, you will be positioned to defy the odds. By learning the power of Both/And thinking, you'll be equipped to craft a story of change that is not only successful, but also sustainable and fulfilling.

Let this be the moment where your journey of successfully leading change begins.

CHAPTER 2

THE PROGRESS PARADOX

Embracing Innovation AND Consistency

INNOVATION — *The deliberate choice to introduce something new or try something in a different way. It's the ability to translate ideas and opportunities into improvements and advancements.*

CONSISTENCY — *The commitment to proven processes and established plans that have a track record of effectiveness and success. It is the dedication to understand, value, and leverage what works.*

STEP 1: UNDERSTAND

Mastering the art of leveraging both innovation and consistency is crucial for leaders, teams, and organizations seeking long-term success. As the following graphic illustrates, there are positive results that come exclusively from focusing on both. At the same time, there are inevitable negative results if you overfocus on one value to the neglect of the other.

TENSION
Embracing Innovation AND Consistency

POSITIVE RESULTS OF
EMBRACING INNOVATION

- Capitalizes on new opportunities, processes, and technologies
- Increases staff excitement, focus, and commitment
- Stay relevant and become known as an industry trailblazer

POSITIVE RESULTS OF
EMBRACING CONSISTENCY

- Harnesses proven processes for quality and efficiency
- Cultivates a confident and competent workforce
- Establishes a positive, trusted reputation

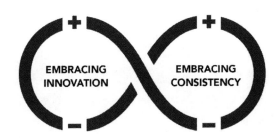

EMBRACING INNOVATION

EMBRACING CONSISTENCY

NEGATIVE RESULTS
WHEN **OVERDONE**

- Lose grip on best practices and solid reputation
- Constant disruption leads to burnout and team dysfunction
- Risky choices result in mistakes and long-term failure

NEGATIVE RESULTS
WHEN **OVERDONE**

- Become risk-averse and miss out on opportunities
- Staff become disengaged and resistant to change
- Stagnant and outdated practices lead to irrelevance

Based on the Polarity Map® and Principles of Barry Johnson and Polarity Partnerships LLC

STEP 2: ASSESS

As you reflect on recent months, consider your team's openness to innovation—embracing new ideas and methods. At the same time, have you effectively leveraged proven strategies and upheld the core strengths you're recognized for?

Examine the following assessment to determine which quadrant best represents where your team has focused its efforts.

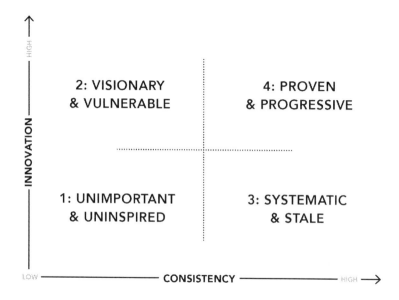

STEP 3: LEVERAGE

No matter what quadrant you currently find yourself in the most, the goal is to spend more time in quadrant four in the season ahead. The exciting part? There are actionable steps you can take to make this a reality. By implementing the following ideas, you'll harness the benefits of *both* innovation *and* consistency, establishing yourself as both proven and progressive.

EMBRACING INNOVATION

"It's easy to come up with new ideas; the hard part is letting go of what worked for you two years ago but will soon be out of date."

– ROGER VON OECH

AUTHOR AND CREATIVITY GURU

1. Discuss the deltas.

When I began my career as a corporate trainer, I had the privilege of working alongside Fred Clark, a talented leader and instructor. Together, we led corporate clients through outdoor team-building and adventure-based training on high ropes courses.

One practice Fred instilled in our team stands out vividly to me still, decades later: the "Plus/Delta Debrief." After each program, regardless of the amount of cleanup that awaited us, Fred would gather the team for a brief conversation. Facing one another in a circle, we'd start with the "plusses," acknowledging what went well during our program and how to build on those successes in the future. Then, we'd focus on what we might try differently next time. We referred to these as our "deltas" as we discussed opportunities for change.

These delta conversations were invaluable. They weren't about dwelling on failures but rather about identifying opportunities for refinement. Even when things went incredibly well, we still consistently generated ideas that might lead to improvement.

By framing these discussions as plusses and deltas as opposed to taking a traditional pros and cons approach, we fostered a culture of healthy challenge. It was empowering—we felt motivated to explore new ideas and approaches without feeling defeated or embarrassed.

This technique isn't limited to outdoor adventures; it works for any organization. Taking a page from Fred's playbook, carve out time for this type of reflection, both as a team and individually. This discipline is a sure way to foster a growth mindset throughout your team as you embrace change with the confidence that you are one step closer to excellence.

By integrating regular Plus/Delta Debriefs into your team's routine, you will quickly gain the benefits of innovation and continuous improvement.

2. Make good mistakes.

Fostering a culture of innovation means being comfortable with making mistakes and occasionally experiencing failure. However, this doesn't entail being irresponsible or adopting a laissez-faire attitude towards quality and commitments. It's about embracing what author and scholar Amy Edmondson calls "the right kind of wrong"—a distinction between detrimental failures to avoid and "intelligent failures" that offer valuable opportunities for learning and growth.[1]

Edmondson's work highlights that not all failures are harmful; intelligent failures that occur within experimentation and exploration are essential for organizational innovation. This healthy kind of failure brings you new information, and as you discover paths that don't work, you ultimately find the paths that do work and claim new territory you would've otherwise missed.

While these intelligent failures are inevitable within an innovative culture, they must be managed carefully to minimize risks. Edmondson advocates for creating environments within teams and organizations where new ideas can be piloted without the fear of catastrophic consequences. These environments encourage calculated risk-taking with a commitment to learning and adapting from each experience, whether it results in success or temporary setbacks.

Edmondson not only differentiates between detrimental failures, which should be avoided, and intelligent failures, which should be expected, but she also stresses the importance of team members understanding the distinction between good and bad mistakes. She labels these as "blameworthy mistakes" versus "praiseworthy mistakes."[2]

High-performance teams do not tolerate blameworthy mistakes that result from factors like inattention, lack of ability, or deviance. However, they actively celebrate mistakes arising from the courage to embrace complexity, hypothesis testing, and experimentation in pursuit of goals. When teams recognize that certain mistakes are unacceptable while others are crucial for fostering an innovative culture, they become more willing to take the right kind of risks while being responsible at the same time.

By applying Edmondson's principles to foster a culture that values learning from the right kind of failures and mistakes, you and your team can unlock the transformative potential of innovation and change.

EMBRACING CONSISTENCY

"People think focus means saying yes to the thing you've got to focus on. But that's not what it means at all. It means saying no to the hundred other good ideas that there are. You have to pick carefully."

– STEVE JOBS

CO-FOUNDER AND FORMER CEO OF APPLE INC.

1. Focus on what works.

When you are learning to drive, one of the first lessons you're taught is to focus on where you want to go, not where you want to avoid. If you're fixated on the guardrail or the ditch, you'll inevitably veer in that direction. Similarly, in your professional endeavours, if you concentrate too much on what's not working, you risk ignoring what is actually working well and potentially heading in the wrong direction.

Appreciative Inquiry[3] offers a powerful way to identify and study what's working at its very best, enabling you to replicate those successes in the future. This interactive process works like a magnifying glass, bringing into focus where individuals and teams are currently excelling. By recognizing and repeating best practices, it allows organizations to capture the upsides of consistency and tradition, ensuring past successes become the new normal moving forward.

To tap into the power of Appreciative Inquiry within your team, carve out time at your next meeting to work through the following three steps:

1. **Share success stories.** Give each team member time to share a recent, specific instance when things were working at their very best. These stories can focus on teamwork, breakthroughs, or accomplishments.

2. **Listen to understand.** Encourage curious and active listening when each story is shared. Team members are encouraged to ask clarifying questions so they fully understand not only *what* happened, but *how* it happened.

3. **Strategize together.** After each success story, transition into a group discussion around how this best-case scenario can be replicated in the season ahead.

Appreciative Inquiry fosters actionable and collaborative team engagement around identifying what works and strategizing how to sustain these achievements in the future. It's a positive and motivating way to ensure your team holds on to the value of consistency.

2. Look away!

Shiny Object Syndrome (SOS) is the tendency for individuals to gravitate toward novel and trendy ideas or opportunities, often at the expense of their current objectives. Fueled by a fear of missing out and a craving for excitement, this phenomenon can result in a loss of focus and neglect of long-term goals.

As an entrepreneur and business owner, I'm especially vulnerable to SOS due to my hard-wired optimism and enthusiasm for new ideas. However, I've come to realize through experience that while many of these opportunities appear enticing, pursuing them impulsively can derail progress and hinder my overall success.

Recognizing and managing SOS are essential for benefiting from consistency within my organization. It's important that I acknowledge when I'm being drawn away by the allure of a slick, new idea and, instead, maintain focus on my current priorities and stay committed to my long-term objectives.

To minimize the downsides of SOS within your team, it's helpful to utilize a powerful question introduced by author and business strategist Greg McKeown: "If we were to say yes to this new, novel idea or opportunity, what will we have to say no to? And are we okay with that?"[4] This question helps to distinguish between mere distractions and genuine innovations by forcing you to consider the trade-offs.

Personally, I've discovered that discussing this question with my team can be game changing. It allows me to see potential downsides and manage the blind spots created by SOS.

LET YOUR MISSION GUIDE YOU

When you think of some of the most successful and respected brands, one common thread emerges: the ability to successfully manage the tension between innovation and consistency. The Walt Disney Company, renowned for its timeless animated films and theme parks, has skillfully ventured into new territory such as cable networks and streaming platforms to adapt to evolving audience preferences. Similarly, Coca-Cola has maintained its iconic brand image and product consistency while introducing innovative flavours, packaging, and market expansions (e.g., Powerade, SmartWater) to remain relevant and competitive in the beverage industry.

These organizations demonstrate a willingness to embrace risks and explore new ideas yet remain unwavering in their commitment to their mission. For over a century, Disney has been dedicated to its mission of "entertaining, informing, and inspiring people around the globe through the power of unparalleled storytelling." Likewise, for over 130 years, Coca-Cola has remained true to its vision of "crafting brands and providing drink choices that people love, refreshing them in body and spirit."

These mission statements aren't mere wall decorations; they serve as a North Star directing the organization's every action. While their pursuit of innovation may not always follow a straight path, an alignment to their mission ensures they are always going in the right direction. New ideas that are consistent with the mission become acceptable while innovations outside of these boundaries are considered distractions and inefficient uses of time and resources.

So, in the wise words of author and speaker Simon Sinek, begin by clarifying your *why*, replicate successful strategies aligned with this purpose, and take calculated risks to ensure your *how* remains current and competitive.[5]

CHAPTER 3

KNOWING IT VERSUS EXPERIENCING IT

Validating Facts AND Feelings

FACTS — *Information, evidence, and strategy that paint a clear picture of the why, how, and when, legitimizing the need for change and instilling confidence moving forward.*

FEELINGS — *The emotional rollercoaster individuals ride when navigating change, regardless of their understanding of the change.*

STEP 1: UNDERSTAND

F inding healthy tension between facts and feelings is essential for leaders, teams, and organizations striving to lead change successfully. As illustrated in the following graphic, there are distinct benefits resulting from acknowledging and incorporating both. At the same time, overfocusing on one while neglecting the other is a recipe for disaster.

TENSION
Validating Facts AND Feelings

POSITIVE RESULTS OF
VALIDATING FACTS

- Increases organizational confidence and trust
- Fosters clarity and alignment among team members
- Enhances implementation and decision-making

POSITIVE RESULTS OF
VALIDATING FEELINGS

- Builds stronger relationships and trust among team members
- Empowers individuals to express concerns and opinions
- Facilitates smoother acceptance and adoption

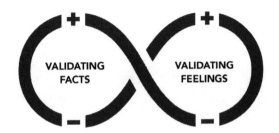

NEGATIVE RESULTS
WHEN **OVERDONE**

- Deteriorates relationships and team morale
- Increases anxiety and stress among team members
- Lack of empathy leads to decreased engagement

NEGATIVE RESULTS
WHEN **OVERDONE**

- Decreases confidence in leadership and decision-making
- Fails to develop resilience in team members
- Delays implementation and creates missed opportunities

STEP 2: ASSESS

Reflect on some recent changes and assess the extent to which you have validated both facts and feelings within your team. Have you balanced the reliance on data and evidence with acknowledging and addressing the emotional aspects of change?

Review the assessment below and identify the quadrant that best illustrates how your team is managing the tension between facts and feelings.

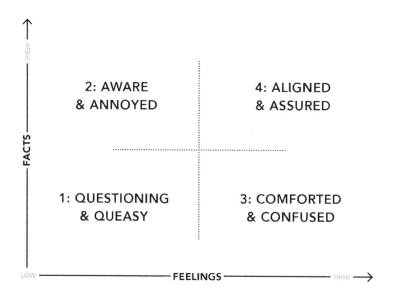

STEP 3: LEVERAGE

In the upcoming season, the goal is to spend more time in quadrant four. The good news? There are practical strategies you can implement to make this goal a reality. By putting the following ideas into action, you'll harness the advantages of focusing on *both* facts *and* feelings, paving the way for change management success.

VALIDATING FACTS

1. Clarify the why.

In my decades of experience in organizational development, one book consistently stands out as a cornerstone in change management—the 1996 classic, *Leading Change*,[1] by John Kotter, a professor at Harvard Business School and a renowned expert in the field. In this influential work, Kotter presents an eight-step process for effectively implementing change within organizations.

The first step in Kotter's model emphasizes the critical importance of creating a sense of urgency. For change initiatives to be successful and sustainable, there needs to be a genuine and widespread desire for change throughout the organization. People need to clearly understand why things must change and agree with the rationale. By highlighting key facts and leveraging compelling evidence, leaders can ignite a sense of urgency that motivates individuals to actively support the change effort.

During this early season of change management, Kotter emphasizes the critical role of leadership buy-in, suggesting that at least 75% of management must endorse the change for it to succeed. This means that smart leaders prioritize cultivating a sense of urgency among their peers before cascading it throughout the organization.

Instilling urgency goes beyond merely presenting dismal sales figures or acknowledging heightened competition. It requires open and vulnerable discussions and healthy debate about market dynamics and competitive landscapes. It provides people with simple yet compelling data needed to truly understand potential threats and identify realistic opportunities. Ideally, it includes validation from customers, external partners, and industry experts to increase the credibility of the urgency message.

While creating a sense of urgency, it's critical to avoid a common mistake: painting an overly bleak picture of current reality. This approach often backfires, as it inadvertently places blame on individuals and triggers feelings of defensiveness or embarrassment. This is a surefire way to ramp up resistance.

Instead, the aim should be to acknowledge current successes and the strengths that have brought the organization to its present position while at the same time demonstrating the need for adaptation in response to emerging threats and opportunities.

By striking this balance, you can effectively convey the message that while current strategies may have served the company well in the past, they are no longer sufficient in the face of evolving challenges. This allows you to inspire action by illustrating how embracing change presents the opportunity to achieve even greater success in the future.*

2. Embrace apprehensions.

In the initial chapter, we encountered Disgruntled Dana, Resistant Raj, and Confused Chris, each wrestling with their apprehensions surrounding change. These concerns typically stem from perceived risks, potential losses, or gaps in the proposed strategy. Staying ahead in the change management game requires a proactive approach to address these concerns head-on with concrete, verifiable facts.

When you empathetically acknowledge individuals' concerns, you validate their wisdom in being cautious. And by acknowledging

---

* More information on how to navigate the tension between acknowledging what's been working and demonstrating what needs to change can be found in Chapter 7.

these apprehensions in a confident and informed manner, you foster trust and understanding. This approach dispels any notion that you are naïve or unaware of the challenges ahead.

In some cases, you can also present facts and evidence to demonstrate that people's concerns are unfounded. It's crucial to handle this delicately, avoiding any implication of ignorance or reason for embarrassment on their part. The goal is to offer a compelling narrative based on objective facts and evidence that counteracts what people may perceive as wishful thinking or rose-coloured glasses.

It's not enough to merely address concerns as they arise. You must actively seek out these apprehensions, listening attentively to understand their root causes. Don't write off Dana, Raj, and Chris as mere resisters or people who "just aren't getting it." Instead, have the courage and humility to acknowledge that they may hold valuable wisdom and insights you could benefit from to manage change more effectively.

Turning resisters into change agents hinges on your ability to validate inevitable concerns and challenges and provide evidence-based solutions. This proactive approach not only minimizes resistance but ultimately cultivates a culture of confidence and collective buy-in, propelling the change process forward.

VALIDATING FEELINGS

"Resistance towards change isn't just a case of people being difficult—it's a natural psychological response towards the unknown. More than being tolerated, resistance should be expected and planned for. It's your job to guide people through that transition."

– WILLIAM BRIDGES

AUTHOR, SPEAKER, AND ORGANIZATIONAL CONSULTANT

1. Recognize that good change still feels bad.

Why is it that, at times, the need for change is blatantly clear, people understand the *why* behind the change, and they also grasp the clear strategy to navigate the change successfully, yet you still get resistance? Why do you still feel that people are angry about the change and maybe even at *you* for making them navigate the change? If the *why, how,* and *when* (the facts) are super clear, why do people still resist and fight you moving forward?

Daniel Goleman's research on emotional intelligence[2] sheds light on this dilemma, suggesting that we actually have two brains: a thinking brain and a feeling brain. While the front of our brain (the prefrontal cortex) oversees logic and reason, the back part of our brain (the amygdala) serves as the hub of our emotions and emotional memory.

In times of fear and anxiety, such as during periods of change and uncertainty, our emotional brain can take control, shutting down things like logic, reason, and empathy. This often results in attitudes, opinions, and responses that may be inconsistent with our usual demeanor and values. It's a classic case of emotional hijacking in which our primal reactions take control, leading to resistance and pushback against change initiatives, even when we understand their necessity and rationale.

In other words, it's perfectly normal not to feel upbeat about change—even good change; however, the goal is to minimize these emotional hijacks as much as possible. This doesn't mean shutting down our emotions but rather acknowledging them, understanding what's triggering them, and determining what we need to do to "wake up" our logical brain. Doing so can prevent us from saying or doing things that we'll regret.

This is when the power of caring leadership and team support comes into play. When everyone recognizes the emotional challenges of change, they can rally around each other, offering understanding and encouragement during moments of frustration and stress. This is also when leaders need to check in more frequently at a one-on-one level with their team members to see where they're at emotionally and to explore how to support them when they're struggling with the change.

2. Acknowledge the sense of loss involved in change.

Another reason why good change can still produce negative feelings is rooted in the research of Elisabeth Kübler-Ross[3] whose ground-breaking work on grief highlights the predictability of human responses to loss. Initially applied to individuals coping with the loss of a loved one, her findings have been expanded to encompass responses to significant changes, including those in the workplace.

Denial and shock often mark the initial stage as individuals grapple with the stark reality of change and yearn for the familiarity of the past. Anger and frustration typically follow, sometimes directed outwardly at those perceived to be responsible for the change and sometimes directed inwardly as people feel frustrated with themselves for struggling to adapt. The messy phase of bargaining comes next as individuals try to reconcile the old with the new, experimenting with new strategies and techniques as they navigate the transition. Eventually, the final phase of acceptance signals a commitment to moving forward and embracing the new reality.

While this progression isn't always linear or uniform, it's both predictable and expected because it's linked to the human capacity for resilience and adaptation. Effective leaders recognize and validate these emotional responses to change as they guide their teams through challenging times.

It's important to remember that while experiencing these emotions is completely normal, it's not an excuse to get stuck. Being in denial or feeling angry is normal, but refusing to accept new ways of doing things and staying angry is not okay. The key question to ask is, "How do we accommodate all of these emotional stages while simultaneously moving through them in a healthy way?"

> *"Our ability to manage change hinges on our ability to manage ourselves, including our fears and anxieties. These factors drive everything else—in business and in life."*
>
> **– APRIL RINNE**
> *AUTHOR, FUTURIST, AND ADVISOR*

3. Attend to your own feelings.

Leading change is further complicated by the fact that managers and supervisors often find themselves grappling with the same emotions they seek to help others manage. Despite your enthusiasm for the change, you may still experience moments of anger and frustration as well as a longing for the past. As a leader navigating your own emotional journey—from denial to acceptance—you must create a supportive environment for your own learning, processing, and adapting.

By fostering open communication, providing empathetic support, and leading by example, you can guide your team through the emotional complexities of change, emerging stronger and more cohesive on the other side.

BRAVING THE WILDERNESS

As I reflect on one of my earliest leadership roles as a foreman in a tree-planting company, I'm reminded of the importance of validating *both* facts *and* feelings when navigating change. In the rugged landscapes of northern Canada, many university students are drawn to summer jobs as tree planters due to the potential for high income in a short amount of time. However, this means enduring gruelling labour, sleeping in a tent for two months, and living far from civilization. Predictably, turnover in this industry is exceptionally high. During my first season as a tree planter, my crew of 27 dwindled to just seven by the first day off.

As a foreman, my main goal was to assemble a crew of tree planters who I believed would excel at the job and stick with it. Once the planting season began, it was extremely challenging to replace any staff who quit, so finding the right people was crucial. This meant I had to focus heavily on providing them with all the facts up front. My newly hired crew members were about to undergo one of the most significant changes in their lives with this job, and I wanted to ensure they were well prepared. So I provided them with details about where they would be planting, how piece-rate pay works, tips for thriving in the Canadian wilderness, what essentials to bring, and a breakdown of their daily, weekly, and monthly schedules.

While providing information and facts was helpful, it wasn't enough to retain my crew. I quickly realized that focusing on feelings was equally if not more important. I knew they would face long days of battling snow, rain, and scorching heat while contending with blackflies, mosquitoes, and the threat of bears.

The physical demands of the job were daunting, and I anticipated that their emotions would often get the best of them.

Understanding that they might question why they were enduring such hardships, I made it a priority to routinely check in with each person, especially during the initial weeks. I reassured them that their struggles were normal and expected, offering support and optimism that their efforts would pay off in the end. Additionally, I facilitated team discussions to explore our collective experiences and brainstorm ways to support one another, particularly on challenging days.

Despite a few team members quitting, my crew's retention rate surpassed that of any other crew in our camp. Their dedication was evident as they remained with me for two more seasons before I finally hung up my shovel. Being recognized as one of the top crews in the company reinforced my belief that my approach, focusing on *both* the facts *and* the feelings associated with significant change, was the secret to our success.

CHAPTER 4

SEIZING TODAY, SHAPING TOMORROW

Focusing on the Short Term AND the Long Term

SHORT TERM — *Immediate goals, actions, and innovations driven by taking advantage of real-time opportunities and avoiding imminent threats.*

LONG TERM — *Strategies guided and aligned with vision and core values and aimed at fostering sustained growth and securing organizational success over the long haul.*

STEP 1: UNDERSTAND

Taking advantage of short-term opportunities while holding on to long-term strategy and vision is vital for leaders, teams, and organizations as they navigate change. As depicted in the following graphic, there are clear advantages to embracing both perspectives. However, leaning too heavily towards one while neglecting the other will lead to inevitable challenges and setbacks.

TENSION
Focusing on the Short Term AND the Long Term

POSITIVE RESULTS OF
FOCUSING ON THE SHORT TERM

- Seizing new opportunities and maintaining relevance
- Adapting swiftly to unexpected challenges and threats
- Fostering an agile and dynamic team culture

POSITIVE RESULTS OF
FOCUSING ON THE LONG TERM

- Maintaining alignment with mission, vision, and values
- Prioritizing sustainability, reputation, and enduring success
- Avoiding hasty decisions that lead to regret

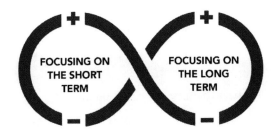

FOCUSING ON THE SHORT TERM

FOCUSING ON THE LONG TERM

NEGATIVE RESULTS
WHEN **OVERDONE**

- Losing sight of long-term goals and strategic direction
- Building unsustainable practices or solutions
- Confusion regarding organizational identity and offerings

NEGATIVE RESULTS
WHEN **OVERDONE**

- Missing out on emerging opportunities or trends
- Losing relevance and failing to evolve with changing landscapes
- Inability to effectively address short-term challenges and threats

STEP 2: ASSESS

Reflect on recent changes and evaluate how well you've embraced *both* short-term *and* long-term considerations within your team. Have you appropriately balanced the immediate goals with the overarching vision? Have you addressed the urgency of short-term needs while keeping sight of long-term strategic objectives?

Review the assessment below and determine which quadrant best describes your team's approach to navigating the tension between the short term and long term.

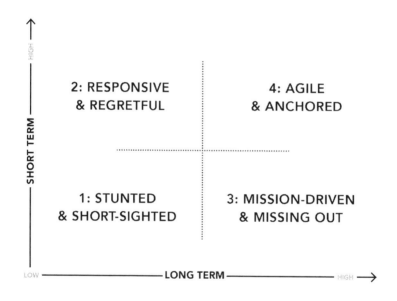

STEP 3: LEVERAGE

No one spends all of their time in quadrant four, but the goal is to constantly increase the amount of time you and your team are residing there. Below are actionable steps to help you achieve this goal. By implementing these strategies, you'll tap into the healthy tension between focusing on the short term and the long term, ensuring effective change management.

FOCUSING ON THE SHORT TERM

"Without short-term wins, too many employees give up or actively join the resistance."

– JOHN KOTTER

HARVARD PROFESSOR, AUTHOR, AND THOUGHT-LEADER

1. Open your eyes.

When leaders prioritize long-term thinking and strategy over seizing immediate opportunities and addressing unexpected threats, they not only risk missing out on short-term gains, but they also leave themselves vulnerable. To address this, you (and ideally, your team) should work through the following questions:

- **Are we flexible?**

  » Is our long-term vision and strategic plan flexible enough to accommodate short-term opportunities and adaptations? How do we know this?

  » Can we provide concrete examples where our long-term vision allowed us to pivot in response to short-term opportunities or challenges?

  » Who was involved in making these decisions, and how did their roles contribute to the healthy flexibility of our strategy?

- **Are we aware?**

  » Are we regularly scanning the environment for emerging trends, threats, and opportunities that may require immediate action?

  » How do we (or could we) conduct this environmental scan?

  » Who is responsible for monitoring different aspects of the environment, and how do they communicate potential opportunities or threats to the leadership team?

- **Are we sure?**

  » Do we have a mechanism in place for quickly evaluating and prioritizing short-term opportunities based on their alignment with our long-term goals?

  » Can we outline the steps of this evaluation process?

- **Are we supportive?**

  » Are we fostering a culture that encourages and rewards agility and responsiveness to changing circumstances?

  » Are we empowering team members at all levels to identify and pursue short-term opportunities that align with our overarching goals? Can we provide specific examples of this?

  » How do leaders model these behaviours, and how are they developed and reinforced throughout the organization?

- **Are we ready?**

  » Do we have the necessary resources and capabilities to capitalize on short-term opportunities without sacrificing our long-term sustainability?

  » Can we identify instances in the past year where this has happened successfully?

  » How do we ensure resource allocation aligns with short-term needs and long-term goals?

- **Are we Both/And?**

  » Are we striking a balance between *both* short-term wins *and* long-term strategic initiatives to ensure sustained success over time?

  » How do we define this balance, and how do we measure our success in achieving it?

  » Can we identify areas where we may need to recalibrate our focus to achieve a more balanced approach between short-term and long-term priorities?

2. Plan out next steps.

Based on the insights from this discussion, explore ways to maintain your long-term values while also adapting to short-term opportunities and challenges in the season ahead. What are a few things you can start doing, stop doing, or continue doing to take advantage of what might be right in front of you?

FOCUSING ON THE LONG TERM

1. "Do" diligence!

When leaders and organizations have a bias towards seizing immediate opportunities and tackling unexpected threats, they may inadvertently jeopardize sustained success in pursuit of short-term gains. If you recognize this tendency within your approach and are on the verge of greenlighting a new change, it's essential to pause and reflect on the following questions. Whether you answer them individually or with your team, they will guide you in ensuring that your short-term bias doesn't negatively impact the long-term vision.

- **Do we have mission alignment?**

  » How does this change align with our organization's long-term vision and strategic plan?

  » What measures can we implement to maintain alignment with our overarching goals?

  » How do we (or could we) effectively communicate the purpose and rationale behind this short-term change in the context of our organization's long-term objectives and values?

- **Do we know the potential pitfalls?**

  » What potential long-term impacts might this short-term change have on our organization?

  » How can we anticipate and mitigate any negative consequences that may arise over time?

» Have we actively sought out perspectives from individuals and stakeholders with a long-term bias to challenge and provide pushback against this change?

- **Do we have better options?**

    » Have we explored alternative approaches that may better serve our organization's long-term interests?

    » How can we ensure that our decision-making process considers a range of options to optimize long-term outcomes?

- **Are we creating capacity issues?**

    » Are we adequately prepared to sustain the success of this short-term change in the long term, considering the ongoing time, energy, and staffing commitments it may require?

    » How will we ensure that resources are allocated effectively to maintain its momentum and impact over time?

- **Are we creating chaos and confusion?**

    » How could this short-term change lead to internal confusion regarding our organizational priorities and values? Externally, how might it obscure our offerings and brand identity?

    » What strategies can we implement to minimize any enduring effects on our values, reputation, and brand recognition, both internally and externally?

2. Plan out next steps.

Based on what you and your team learn from this discussion, explore ways you can seize short-term opportunities that align with your long-term strategy in the season ahead. What are a few things you can start doing, stop doing, or continue doing to stay focused on your mission, vision, and values?

BONUS: FOCUS ON THE SHORT TERM *AND* LONG TERM SIMULTANEOUSLY

"Change is hard because people wear themselves out.
What looks like laziness is often exhaustion."

– CHIP HEATH

PROFESSOR AND NY TIMES BESTSELLING AUTHOR

1. Celebrate wins.

To ensure the sustained success of long-term change initiatives, it's crucial to acknowledge and celebrate short-term victories along the journey. Breaking down the change into manageable milestones transforms the experience from an intimidating ultra-marathon to a series of achievable sprints, each with a visible finish line. These bite-sized achievements not only show progress but also serve as vital morale boosters, especially during seasons where feelings of discouragement and exhaustion prevail.

By embracing and highlighting these mini successes and emphasizing the significance of each step forward, leaders can reinvigorate their teams. This approach not only fosters a sense of accomplishment but also nurtures a culture of resilience and adaptability, essential qualities for navigating complex and evolving landscapes. Ultimately, valuing and celebrating short-term wins reinforces the organization's commitment to long-term objectives while empowering teams to remain motivated and focused at every stage.

PANDEMIC WISDOM (AND WARNINGS)

In reflecting on the recent experience of navigating the global COVID-19 pandemic and observing the diverse responses of organizations, it becomes evident that finding healthy tension between a short-term and long-term focus is vital for effective leadership and organizational success in times of change.

The pandemic served as a litmus test, illuminating the consequences of overemphasizing either end of the spectrum. Some organizations, driven by immediate survival instincts, swiftly pivoted and adapted their operations to meet emergent challenges, seize unexpected revenue streams, and capitalize on government funding opportunities. However, many of those now find themselves grappling with the aftermath of unsustainable business models and confused customer perceptions.

Conversely, those who remained unwavering in their belief that the storm would soon pass failed to recognize the permanent shifts in the landscape, leading to missed opportunities and, in some cases, irrelevance.

Amidst these cautionary tales, there were those who embraced the wisdom of taking a Both/And approach with short-term agility and long-term vision. In the words of Winston Churchill, they "[refused to] let a good crisis go to waste" and leveraged the pandemic as an opportunity for innovation and growth. At the same time, they kept their mission, vision, and values front and centre, remaining unwavering in their strategic objectives. By aligning every short-term decision with their long-term commitment, these organizations not only weathered the storm but emerged stronger and more resilient than before.

In times of change, it is not merely survival but thriving that distinguishes those who harness the power of *both* the short term *and* the long term.

CHAPTER 5

FROM ROADMAPS TO REALITY

Promoting Planning AND Action

PLANNING — *Processing and preparing a clear and confident strategy for change. It involves analyzing scenarios, setting objectives, and ensuring alignment.*

ACTION — *The dynamic process of putting plans into motion with adaptability and agility. It involves aligning the idealistic with the realistic.*

STEP 1: UNDERSTAND

In order to successfully lead change, promoting *both* planning *and* action is critical for leaders, teams, and organizations. It's about valuing and leveraging the advantages of both perspectives while avoiding the pitfalls that come with favouring one over the other. As the graphic below illustrates, there are positive results that can only come from embracing each side, and there are negative results that are inevitable if you overfocus on one side to the neglect of the other.

TENSION
Promoting Planning AND Action

POSITIVE RESULTS OF
PROMOTING PLANNING

- Increases confidence and clarity
- Ensures alignment among individuals and teams
- Reduces mistakes by anticipating challenges

POSITIVE RESULTS OF
PROMOTING ACTION

- Creates momentum
- Responds to unexpected opportunities and threats
- Increases team engagement and learning

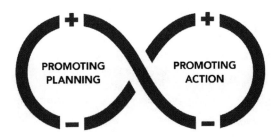

NEGATIVE RESULTS
WHEN **OVERDONE**

- Analysis paralysis stunts progress
- Inability to adapt to changing landscapes
- Rigidity undermines team morale and buy-in

NEGATIVE RESULTS
WHEN **OVERDONE**

- Reactive decisions heighten vulnerability
- Increases fragmented efforts and misalignment
- Escalates team confusion and frustration

STEP 2: ASSESS

Reflect on the past season. When it comes to change, have you reaped the rewards of strategic and thorough planning? Have you also embraced the advantages that come from courageously taking action?

Consider the following chart and evaluate which of the four quadrants you (and your team) are spending the most time in these days.

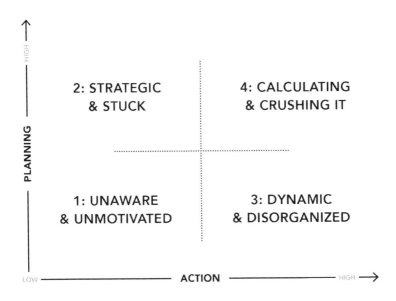

STEP 3: LEVERAGE

Regardless of your current quadrant, the aim is to increase time spent in quadrant four. The good news is it's possible to experience the benefits of *both* planning *and* action when leading change. Here are some simple yet significant actions you can take to ensure your team is both calculated and crushing it.

PROMOTING PLANNING

"Plans are immensely reassuring to most people, not just because they contain information but because they exist."

– WILLIAM BRIDGES

AUTHOR, SPEAKER, AND ORGANIZATIONAL CONSULTANT

1. Plan for confidence.

In times of change, uncertainty often casts shadows of doubt and anxiety. Now more than ever, people turn to their leaders for guidance, seeking reassurance as they navigate the unknown. This is where having a plan—a beacon of hope and stability during the stormy seas of change—becomes vital.

Consider the experience of some close friends of mine who faced a somewhat overwhelming decision concerning their daughter's health. Confronted with her significant medical issue, they were inundated with a myriad of opinions and treatment options from doctors and specialists. The weight of their decision hung heavily upon them, knowing that their daughter's future would be forever impacted.

One day, my friend shared with me that they had made their decision and were moving forward with surgery. When I inquired about their decision-making process and why they chose this path, my friend confessed that the doctor they selected was the only one who presented a clear plan. He admitted that he wasn't sure if it was the best or "right" plan, but it gave both him and his wife the sense of direction and confidence they needed.

This story demonstrates the crucial role of leadership in providing a clear strategy during times of change. Even if the plan acknowledges uncertainties, its mere existence instills confidence in those navigating uncharted territory. It offers a sense of security to those feeling lost.

As a leader, it's imperative you communicate not only the existence of a plan but also its rationale and soundness. You cannot overdo this! By laying out a sensible plan, you empower your team to navigate change with confidence and resilience. In the face of uncertainty, a well-crafted plan serves as a lifeline, guiding individuals through the unpredictable terrain of change and transformation.

2. Go slow to go fast.

In the whirlwind of today's fast-paced work environment where speed and efficiency seem to win the day, there's an often-overlooked truth: Sometimes, slowing down is the fastest way forward. This paradoxical wisdom of going slow to go fast is particularly relevant when leading change. By taking the time to develop a thoughtful and thorough plan upfront, you lay the groundwork for smoother implementation, ultimately leading to greater speed and efficiency in the long run.

While it might initially feel counterintuitive to hit the brakes when feeling the urgency of change, taking a deliberate approach offers significant benefits. By investing upfront in gaining clarity and perspective, you equip yourself and your team with the insights needed to navigate challenges effectively. Rather than rushing headlong into uncertain territory, pausing to plan enables you to anticipate obstacles, mitigate risks, and make informed decisions. In doing so, you're empowered to navigate transitions with confidence and precision, striking a balance in which speed complements thoroughness and efficiency is upheld alongside thoughtful consideration.

3. Anticipate learning curves.

Think of a skill you consider yourself great at, whether in your profession, a hobby, or a sport. Now, recall a time when this skill was a new endeavour for you. Undoubtedly, you weren't always so great. You made mistakes, learned through practice and experience, and encountered what is commonly known as a learning curve.

A learning curve is the relationship between your competence in a skill and your level of experience. When tackling something new or innovative, this curve will be steep. It's inevitable. In navigating change, you must recognize this reality and plan accordingly.

During periods of transition and innovation, assume that things may worsen before improving. Team cohesion may waver before strengthening, and productivity might falter before rebounding. A well-crafted plan anticipates these fluctuations, allocating resources, time, and support for navigating the learning curve effectively.

Without anticipating and discussing the unavoidable learning curve with your team, those who are resistant to change will find validation for their resistance, pointing to setbacks as evidence of failure or misdirection. Meanwhile, even those who are initially supportive may succumb to anxiety if unprepared for challenges. However, by proactively addressing the learning curve and integrating it into the plan, you will minimize surprises and equip individuals to face adversity head-on.

PROMOTING ACTION

"Everybody has a plan until they get punched in the face."

– MIKE TYSON

AMERICAN PROFESSIONAL BOXER

1. Let experience be your guide.

Some of the most profound learning experiences in our lives stem not from textbooks we read, lectures we hear, or plans we're given, but from hands-on involvement and just doing it. However, the mere act of experiencing something isn't always sufficient for learning; it requires a deeper level of reflection and inquiry.

I can think of many times in my life where I've made the same mistake over and over again. Why is this? Why do we sometimes learn from experience and other times get stuck in a downward spiral? This is a question that kept researcher David Kolb up at night and ultimately led to the development of his "Experiential Learning Cycle." Kolb's research found that in order to learn from experience, we have to carve out time to ask and reflect on three key questions: What? So What? Now What?[1]

The first stage of the cycle involves reflection on the experience itself. This is referred to as the "What" stage, prompting questions such as:

- What stands out as we transition from strategy to action?
- What unexpected challenges have arisen?
- What aspects are proving effective, and what needs adjustment?

Moving beyond the experience itself, the cycle progresses to the stage of generalization. Here, the focus shifts from "What" to "So What." Drawing on the lessons gained from recent experiences, we begin to identify broader patterns and implications:

- How do these insights apply to future scenarios associated with the change?
- What overarching lessons can we develop from our observations?

Finally, the cycle finishes in the learning application stage, transitioning from "So What" to "Now What." With fresh insights and implications regarding the execution of the change:

- How can we adapt and enhance our plan and actions in real time?
- What adjustments need to be made?
- What strategies should be amplified, and which ones require refinement?

By leveraging these insights, we ensure that our efforts to implement change are not only effective but also sustainable in the long term.

For example, let's say after a year of research and planning, I recently launched a website to promote my keynotes and workshops. During a conversation with a colleague in the United States, I'm surprised when she mentions she didn't consider booking me for her conference because she noticed my website domain ends in .ca instead of .com, and she assumed I only worked in Canada.

This realization prompts the initial "What" stage of reflection. However, I understand that I must delve deeper, and I transition to the "So What" phase. In this case, I begin to generalize that other people might make similar assumptions, not just in the U.S. but also internationally, based on the .ca domain and office address displayed on my webpage.

Recognizing the need for action, I progress to the "Now What" stage. Given my love for international work and to eliminate any ambiguity, I decide to implement a clear banner on each page of my website that states "Delivering Keynotes and Workshops Around the World.".

Effective leaders understand that having a great plan is not enough. When transitioning from planning to action, things won't always work out as expected. The learning curve will result in numerous unexpected challenges. In these moments, it is critical, both individually and as a team, to reflect and ask the What? So What? and Now What? questions. By continuously learning from the experiences of change and adjusting and enhancing the plan as you proceed, you can ensure the best results.

2. State the date.

You've probably heard the popular saying, "Good is the enemy of great." However, when it comes to leading change, "great" can sometimes be the enemy of "good enough for now." And without good enough for now, you'll never get going. Plans can languish in the quest for perfection, never gaining the traction needed to move forward.

Setting and publicly declaring a clear date for action is crucial for creating momentum and ensuring implementation. Without a specific launch date communicated to your team and to stakeholders, change initiatives can easily get postponed indefinitely.

By committing to a date for moving forward, you signal action and accountability.

Consider the example of Apple's launch of the iPhone[2] under the leadership of Steve Jobs. Despite not being entirely ready, at a Macworld event on January 9, 2007, Jobs publicly announced the launch date, setting a bold deadline for action. This decision to move forward with the biggest change in the company's history, even in the face of imperfection, allowed Apple to deliver on its promise and launch the phone less than six months later on June 29. While the iPhone wasn't perfect upon release and required subsequent updates and fixes, Apple's willingness to set a date and take action propelled them to the forefront of innovation, revolutionizing the mobile phone industry.

In the world of change management, setting a date serves as a tangible commitment to progress. It creates a sense of urgency and accountability, driving momentum and ensuring that plans are translated into action. Set a date, declare it to others, and propel your change initiatives forward.

A DOCTOR'S DIAGNOSIS

In the intense environment of the emergency room, the interplay between planning and action isn't just about efficiency—it's a matter of life and death. My friend Joel, a seasoned ER doctor, has shared numerous stories with me, demonstrating the vital importance of both elements.

Take, for instance, the pivotal task of securing an airway in an emergency, which means inserting a breathing tube down someone's trachea so they have enough oxygen. This procedure often involves the patient not breathing for a few moments, so it is extremely important to get it right. After years of rigorous training, doctors like Joel have learned and rehearsed a meticulously planned procedure designed to safeguard their patients' well-being.

However, Joel has recounted moments when swift, decisive action required deviating from the plan. He has made the split-second decision to skip all steps of the algorithm and make an incision in the patient's neck to insert the tube directly into the trachea. This is a rare occurrence, but it can be the difference between life and death.

Joel's insights extend to his role as a mentor for interns, guiding them through the dynamic balance of planning and action in their journey toward becoming proficient doctors. Many interns arrive armed with extensive theoretical knowledge and elaborate plans for every conceivable scenario. Yet, despite their preparation, they often grapple with a sense of unreadiness when confronted with real-life patient care because patients do not always follow the textbook.

Some interns will list all the investigations that they could do for the patient yet are unable to decide what test to actually order. Joel teaches them that the role of an ER doctor includes the "decision point" where one must choose the next step forward. While planning is crucial, this decision point indicates action, which will often determine the patient's outcome.

Conversely, Joel recounts situations with interns who, upon completing their ICU placements, show an unwarranted sense of overconfidence. Despite exposure to a variety of medical conditions, these interns lack the depth of knowledge necessary for comprehensive patient care within the unpredictability of an ER setting.

Being decisive without the full planning and training of a complete residency can be dangerous. It's the idea that "you don't know what you don't know." Joel underscores that true competence requires a methodical, planned approach based on sound medical knowledge instead of narrowly heading down one path only to realize you missed other potential diagnoses.

Joel's experience is a great example of the profound wisdom in embracing *both* planning *and* action. While planning offers direction and confidence, action brings your aspirations to life, propelling you forward in your pursuit of growth and discovery. Whether navigating the complexities of medicine or leading an organizational change, finding healthy tension between planning and action is essential for success.

CHAPTER 6

DECODING CHANGE

Valuing Complexity AND Simplicity

> **COMPLEXITY** — *A thorough analysis and deep understanding of the system or situation that lead to a comprehensive and detailed change management strategy.*

> **SIMPLICITY** — *The art of distilling complex ideas, processes, and strategies into clear, understandable, and actionable concepts.*

STEP 1: UNDERSTAND

Valuing *both* complexity *and* simplicity is essential for leaders, teams, and organizations in order to effectively lead change. This requires recognizing and harnessing the strengths of both approaches while being mindful of the risks associated with favouring one at the expense of the other. As illustrated in the graphic below, there are unique benefits that result from embracing both complexity and simplicity. However, there are also inevitable downsides that you'll experience when one is overemphasized to the neglect of the other.

TENSION
Valuing Complexity AND Simplicity

POSITIVE RESULTS OF
VALUING COMPLEXITY

- Deepens understanding of the situation and the plan
- Increases ability to address emerging challenges and seize opportunities
- Enhances the probability of successful implementation

POSITIVE RESULTS OF
VALUING SIMPLICITY

- Clear, understandable and easy to follow
- Easy to communicate and align teams around
- Reduces confusion among staff and increases overall buy-in

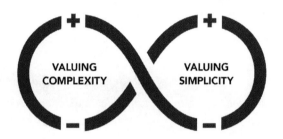

VALUING COMPLEXITY

VALUING SIMPLICITY

NEGATIVE RESULTS
WHEN **OVERDONE**

- People feel overwhelmed and intimidated
- Difficulty in translating complicated plans into practical, actionable steps
- Diminishes excitement and hinders buy-in

NEGATIVE RESULTS
WHEN **OVERDONE**

- Underestimates the significance and nuances of the situation
- Lacks sufficient preparation for handling unforeseen challenges
- Oversimplification hinders successful execution of the plan

STEP 2: ASSESS

Reflect on your recent change management experiences. Have you fully leveraged the advantages that come from leaning into complexity? Have you shown the flexibility required to achieve the benefits of simplicity?

Check out the chart below and determine which quadrant your team has been spending the most time in.

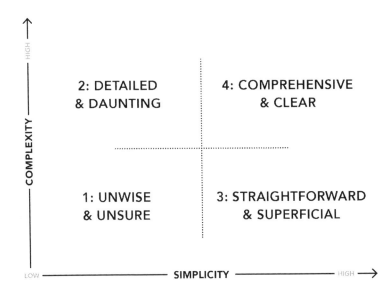

STEP 3: LEVERAGE

Regardless of which quadrant reflects your current situation, the objective is to increasingly operate within the fourth quadrant as you move forward. The encouraging part? There are clear and achievable steps you can take to make this shift. By putting these strategies into practice, you'll capture the advantages of embracing *both* complexity *and* simplicity, allowing you to lead change in a comprehensive and clear way.

VALUING COMPLEXITY

1. Recognize when more is better.

Leveraging complexity in change management requires crafting a strategy that is both multifaceted and meticulously detailed. Fortunately, by getting this far in the book, you are equipped with the essential knowledge to meet this challenge. The objective now is to weave together the insights and wisdom distilled from the previous chapters into a robust change management plan.

From Chapter 2, "Embracing Innovation AND Consistency," you've learned the critical importance of a strategy that honours both change and stability. As you champion an upcoming change—unapologetically articulating the why, the mechanisms of implementation, and the brighter future ahead—remember that it's equally vital to communicate what will remain unchanged. Emphasize your commitment to uphold the organization's core values, maintain its reputation, and sustain the quality standards that define your success.

From Chapter 3, "Validating Facts AND Feelings," you've recognized the essential role of acknowledging both the empirical evidence and the emotional responses that accompany change. As you guide your team through transitions, be sure to present the factual rationale behind the change while also addressing the emotional impact it may have on individuals (regardless of how much it makes sense on paper). By validating both the hard numbers and the human emotions, you create a comprehensive approach that respects the logic of the mind as well as the language of the heart.

From Chapter 4, "Focusing on the Short Term AND the Long Term," you've learned the significance of maintaining a dual focus that captures immediate milestones as well as future aspirations. As you implement change, it's crucial to set short-term goals that yield quick wins and provide tangible evidence of progress. At the same time, it's important to articulate the long-term vision that these immediate steps are building towards. This approach ensures that while the team celebrates early successes, they also remain aligned with the ultimate objectives, keeping motivation high and the end goal in sight.

From Chapter 5, "Promoting Planning AND Action," you've seen the need for leaders to exhibit both comprehensive planning and agile execution. Convey the depth of your strategic planning to instill confidence, highlighting your preparedness for potential challenges. Simultaneously, showcase your agility by swiftly responding to new information and adapting plans in action. This dual demonstration of careful foresight and flexible responsiveness will inspire your team to effectively implement change while remaining adaptable to evolving circumstances.

By incorporating these principles into your change management strategy, you will create a roadmap that not only addresses the complexities of your organization and the situation, but also harnesses them as a source of innovation, empathy, and strategic foresight.

2. Understand that one size does not fit all.

In my previous playbook, *Next-Level Teamwork*, I emphasized the significance of accommodating diverse learning styles to empower individuals effectively. As we navigate the complexities of leading change, this principle becomes even more relevant. A change management strategy must be multifaceted and address the varied ways in which people digest new information and adapt to transformation. Here are the three learning styles covered in that book:

1. **Experimenters** – These are people who learn best by doing. They need to be given the ability to try things out and learn through action.

2. **Imitators** – These are people who learn best by seeing it done well and then replicating it. They gain confidence from coming alongside someone who is skilled and experienced.

3. **Analyzers** – These are people who read the instruction manuals for their TVs and appliances. They love information and need to know all the facts and details in order to be confident.

When leading change, it's essential to craft messages and provide opportunities that resonate with Experimenters, Imitators, and Analyzers alike. Experimenters thrive on the opportunity to engage directly with the new processes, so provide them with safe environments where they can explore the change through hands-on experience.

For Imitators, change is best internalized by observing role models who exemplify the desired behaviours and outcomes of the change initiative. Create opportunities for them to witness these practices in action.

Analyzers, on the other hand, require detailed information and a deep understanding of the rationale behind the change. Arm them with comprehensive resources that explain the facts and data supporting the transition.

By tailoring your change management approach to accommodate all of these learning styles, you ensure that each team member can grasp and contribute to the change process in the way that suits them best. This not only facilitates a smoother transition but also leverages the inherent complexity of change to your organization's advantage.

VALUING SIMPLICITY

"As a useful rule of thumb, whenever you cannot describe the vision driving a change initiative in five minutes or less and get a reaction that signifies both understanding and interest, you are in for trouble."

– JOHN KOTTER

HARVARD PROFESSOR, AUTHOR, AND THOUGHT LEADER

NOTE: *As we move into the power of leveraging simplicity in change management, it is important to recognize the significant influence of Donald Miller's work on this subject. My collaboration with Miller and the StoryBrand team over the years has been nothing short of life-changing, shaping not only the insights in this chapter but also my broader perspective. Miller's ground-breaking work,* Building a StoryBrand,[1] *explores the essence of simplicity and the art of clear communication with unparalleled depth. To truly enrich your understanding of these concepts, I cannot recommend his book enough.*

1. Break the curse of knowledge.

As a leader driving transformative change, you possess a deep well of knowledge and expertise. You've immersed yourself in the intricacies, analyzed the data, and crafted a comprehensive strategy. You have a 10 out of 10 level of comprehension.

However, a critical challenge arises: the "Curse of Knowledge." This cognitive bias, coined by economists Colin Camerer, George

Loewenstein, and Martin Weber,[2] occurs when you assume others share your level of understanding and then fail to recognize or accommodate the knowledge gap that exists.

The reality is, despite your 10/10 level of understanding, when you step away from the boardroom, your staff and stakeholders typically grasp the situation at a basic 2/10 level. Anticipating this knowledge gap, you are committed to simplifying your messaging, aiming to bridge the divide by distilling your comprehensive 10/10 understanding down to that 2/10 level.

However, despite being convinced that you've reached the 2/10 mark, it's quite easy to still communicate at a 7/10 level. And this chasm between the 2/10 level of your audience and your supposedly simplified 7/10 messaging is the Curse of Knowledge. Tragically, most leaders remain unaware of this cognitive bias, blind to the reality that their attempts at simplification still have a long way to go.

The key to overcoming the Curse of Knowledge lies in the art of simplification. It's not about dumbing down the message but rather about meeting your audience where they are, ensuring they can grasp the essence of the change and its impact on their roles. Effective simplification requires empathy and a willingness to step into the shoes of those you're leading. Ask yourself: What are their pain points? What are their concerns? What information do they truly need to know so they can understand and embrace the change?

At the core, people need to know two fundamental things:

1. What problem does this change solve for me?

2. What does this change mean for me in terms of what I can gain or lose?

Once you've identified these crucial elements, craft your communication in a way that resonates with your team's level of understanding. Use analogies, real-world examples, and storytelling techniques to bridge the gap between your expertise and their current knowledge.

Remember, the goal is not to overwhelm with intricate details but to provide a clear, compelling narrative that inspires action and buy-in. By mastering the art of simplification, you can overcome the Curse of Knowledge and lead your team towards successful transformation.

2. Use a three-step plan.

When it comes to simplifying complex ideas and plans, there is a powerful psychological principle that leaders can leverage: the power of three. Our brains have an innate ability to resonate with and remember things presented in threes.

Think about common phrases and instructions ingrained in our minds from childhood: "Stop, Drop, and Roll" for handling fires or dialing 9-1-1 for emergencies. The triadic structure makes them easy to recall and follow.

Research suggests that two-step plans feel incomplete, lacking sufficient detail, while four or more steps can overwhelm and disengage the audience. But a three-step structure strikes the perfect balance, providing just enough information to feel comprehensive yet remain digestible.

When communicating complex change initiatives, leaders often make the mistake of outlining dozens of intricate steps, thinking they are being thorough. However, this level of detail can inadvertently breed resistance and confusion.

The solution? Simplify the complexity into three clear, actionable steps. "First, we will start here. Then, we will do this. Finally, that will lead us to our desired outcome." This triadic structure transforms an overwhelming plan into an understandable and even exciting roadmap.

I witnessed the power of three firsthand during a family adventure in New Zealand. As we approached a stream crossing on an incredibly scenic hike, our risk-averse son quickly declared there was no way he would traverse what he dramatically referred to as a "raging river." Sensing his apprehension, I decided to leverage the power of three.

I calmly outlined a simple three-step plan: "First, you'll walk out on that sandbar just below the surface. Second, you'll hop on that fallen log and carefully walk across it. Finally, you'll jump off the log and use those stepping stones to reach the other side."

Remarkably, as soon as I framed the challenge with three steps, my son's assessment transformed from daunting to achievable. With an enthusiastic, "Oh, I can do that!," he confidently followed the three steps and successfully crossed the stream.

By harnessing the power of three, leaders can turn complex change initiatives into digestible, memorable, and inspiring plans of action. This simple yet profound technique can be the key to unlocking understanding, buy-in, and successful execution.

A HOME. A JOB. A FRIEND.

During my nine years at the helm of a 40-bed homeless shelter, I quickly learned that eradicating homelessness and getting individuals off the streets and into safe, sustainable housing involved staggering complexity. Our change management strategy, which applied to each person who walked through our doors, encompassed a dizzying array of elements—housing, employment, healthcare, community reintegration, education, and at times, addiction, mental health challenges, and past trauma.

The list seemed endless, and here's the harsh truth: every component mattered. There was no silver bullet solution, no easy answer. The path to lasting life change demanded a holistic, personalized approach that wove together all these intricate threads.

As a team, we had to become well-versed—or partner with experts who were well-versed—in each of these areas. However, trying to explain this intricate web of services to those seeking our help was overwhelming for them, even paralyzing. And communicating our model for change to staff and volunteers in a way that inspired understanding, buy-in, and excitement seemed like an insurmountable task.

That's when a mentor and homelessness expert, Dion Oxford, shared a profound truth that changed everything: For individuals to move away from a situation of homelessness, they need three things—a home, a job, and a friend. Deceptively simple yet deeply powerful.

A home didn't necessarily mean home ownership, but it did mean a safe, secure place to experience community. A job might not equate to gainful employment, but it did mean the opportunity to contribute skills and energy in a meaningful way. And a friend represented authentic, supportive relationships, not just a transactional connection with a caseworker.

Suddenly, the overwhelming complexity of our work could be distilled into this incredibly straightforward framework. The 1,000 moving parts all fell under one of the three headings. And once we embraced this simplicity, everything shifted.

Those seeking our services understood the path forward. Staff and volunteers rallied around a shared language and vision. The community grasped our approach, leading to heightened volunteerism, donations, and partnerships. By holding the complexity and simplicity in tension, we unlocked a transformative synergy that propelled our mission forward.

CHAPTER 7

UNLEASHING CHANGE CHAMPIONS

How to Bolster Buy-In AND Build Momentum

HOW CHANGE SAVVY ARE YOU?

We all know that leading change can be messy and rarely goes exactly according to plan. However, understanding the typical responses people have to organizational shifts is helpful for minimizing delays, confusion, and resistance. Remember the universal cast of characters from Chapter 1: Disgruntled Dana, Resistant Raj, Confused Chris, Trailblazing Terry, and Utopian Uma? Inspired by these usual suspects, we can narrow down individuals' typical responses to change into one of three categories:

1. **The Early Adopters** — Early Adopters are enthusiastic champions of change. They embrace new strategies and innovations with excitement, readily supporting the change from the outset. Trailblazing Terry and Utopian Uma fall into this category.

2. **The Resisters** — The Resisters, or tradition-bearers, actively voice opposition to change initiatives. They struggle to recognize the potential benefits and express aversion or skepticism toward management and advocates of change. Disgruntled Dana and Resistant Raj fit into the Resisters category.

3. **The Bystanders** — Bystanders take a neutral stance—they neither object to nor express excitement about organizational changes. They often lack interest because they don't perceive how the change will directly impact their day-to-day responsibilities. Confused Chris is an example of a Bystander.

When reading these three responses, which one would you say best describes you? Wait! Before you're quick to congratulate yourself on being an Early Adopter, let's ground this in real data. Think about how you've responded to the following real-life situations. In each case, were you enthusiastically embracing the change (Early Adopter), skeptically questioning the need for it (Resister), or simply taking a neutral stance (Bystander)?

1. Transitioning from having a landline phone to using only a cell phone

2. Adopting recycling practices

3. Integrating artificial intelligence (AI) into your personal and professional life

4. Embracing remote/hybrid or flexible work arrangements

5. Switching from traditional cable/satellite TV to streaming services like Netflix

6. Embracing e-commerce and online shopping over traditional brick-and-mortar stores

7. Transitioning from physical CDs/DVDs to streaming music

8. Supporting and participating in diversity, equity, and inclusion initiatives in the workplace

9. Adopting online video conferencing platforms like Zoom for meetings and collaboration

10. Decluttering and letting go of old possessions, clothes, etc. from your home/living space

Now that you've put a little more thought into it, are you still the Early Adopter you thought you were? The reality is most of us have exemplified all three responses depending on the situation. We all have a bit of the Resister, the Early Adopter, and the Bystander within us—and that's okay! It's human nature, and this should give us grace when leading others experiencing resistance or confusion.

Leading change and helping people navigate uncertainty is undeniably challenging. There are no magical formulas or miracle cures that will make things go perfectly and effortlessly. However, understanding and implementing the following "Getting Unstuck" process will significantly support you in minimizing resistance, generating buy-in, and building momentum for sustainable transformation within your organization.

GETTING UNSTUCK

Often when leading change initiatives, we find ourselves in a divisive, unproductive tug-of-war. As leaders, we attempt to pull people towards innovation and the new reality, but the harder we try to get them on board, the harder they dig in their heels and resist. We're stuck!

This tug-of-war arises because we mistakenly communicate change as an Either/Or instead of a Both/And. We mistakenly take a change-versus-stability stance rather than embracing a change-AND-stability approach.

Here's how it looks. Typically, we start by communicating what we clearly see—the positive results of change and the negative results of stability:

POSITIVE RESULTS
OF **CHANGE**

- We will leverage emerging opportunities.
- We will stay relevant and ahead of the competition.
- We will tap into an exciting, innovative workplace culture.

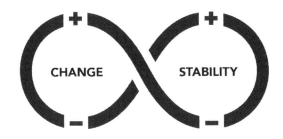

CHANGE   STABILITY

NEGATIVE RESULTS
WHEN **OVERDONE**

- We're missing out on opportunities and falling behind.
- Our lack of relevance will result in business failure.
- We are settling for a boring, uninspired workplace culture.

Meanwhile, the people we are trying to lead see the exact same situation from a very different perspective. What's clear to them are the positive results of stability and the negative results of change:

POSITIVE RESULTS OF STABILITY

- We have established high-quality products and services.
- We have a solid and respected reputation.
- Our team is competent and confident.

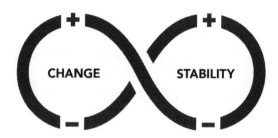

CHANGE   **STABILITY**

NEGATIVE RESULTS WHEN OVERDONE

- Our quality and service will suffer.
- We will confuse clients on who we are and what we do.
- Our team will descend into chaos and confusion.

And what's fascinating—and tragic—is that the clearer we are in communicating the change from an Either/Or perspective, the harder people will resist and pull the other way. This is because, in our attempt to be clear, all people hear is that we don't understand what they value (positive results of stability), and we have no idea of the danger we are pulling them into (negative results of change).

The truth is we are partly right, and they are partly right. But because of the Either/Or approach, both perspectives are incomplete and somewhat wrong.

The only way to get unstuck is to communicate the change in a Both/And way—meaning that as you talk about the opportunities of change, you are just as clear on what's *not* changing and how you will avoid descending into chaos and losing what the team is good at and known for.

So how do you do this? The best strategy is an adaptation of the Getting Unstuck model[1] created by my mentor, Dr. Barry Johnson. It's a powerful way to effectively communicate change so that you maximize buy-in and positive engagement and minimize resistance. Here's how it works:

1. Start by affirming the positive results of stability.

2. Next, validate the potential negative results of change if it's overdone.

3. Then, explore the positive results of change.

4. Finally, discuss how leveraging the positive results of both change and stability helps to achieve a shared higher purpose.

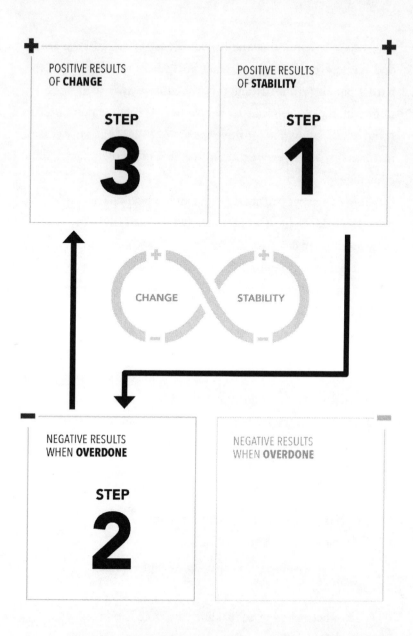

I'm not sure if you noticed it or not, but the one thing you don't need to talk about are the negative results of the current reality, which is normally where leaders mistakenly start. It's not that you can't talk about these at all—some of them might be relevant and important. However, this approach ensures you don't lead with them and damage momentum right from the get-go.

By leveraging the Getting Unstuck model, you overcome the divisive tug-of-war, uncover common ground, and ultimately lead change more effectively. Let's apply the model to a couple of examples.

THE CURRICULUM CONUNDRUM

My wife, Becky, has experienced the change tug-of-war many times as a teacher. It's common for educators to face abrupt over-hauls to long-standing curricula, which at times can feel like a dismissal of their proven expertise. A prime example was the recent province-wide introduction of what was referred to as "the new math," an approach that emphasized creative problem-solving strategies over traditional memorization-based methods.

While the "new math" curriculum update incorporated valu-able research insights, the way it was rolled out unintentionally triggered resistance. The message many teachers and parents received was that the existing math curriculum was outdated and useless and this innovative approach was the only logical path forward.

Not surprisingly, the Either/Or framing of the situation sparked frustration and resistance. Teachers and parents dug in their heels to defend the proven benefits of the existing cur-riculum. They voiced concerns over the perceived abandonment of those fundamentals for an unproven "flavour-of-the-month" pedagogy. The debate even became politically charged with some provincial parties campaigning for a "back-to-basics, com-mon-sense" approach in opposition to new math reforms.

So how could this conundrum have been avoided? How could the curriculum change have been communicated from a Both/ And perspective using the Getting Unstuck approach?

1. **Start by affirming the positive results of stability (what teachers value in the existing approach).** Teachers have incredible expertise with teaching methods that include memorization drills, flash cards, and worksheets that are proven to be effective in helping students master foundational math skills and procedures.

2. **Next, validate the negative results of change if it's overdone (fears around the new curriculum).** An abrupt shift to adopt new strategies understandably raises concerns as it could disrupt students' grasp of core math concepts while creating uncertainty and extra work for educators.

3. **Then, explore the positive results of change (benefits of the new curriculum).** AND research is clearly demonstrating that some new discovery-based strategies are equipping students with innovative and creative problem-solving skills they need for real-world math applications.

4. **Finally, discuss how leveraging the positive results of both change and stability can achieve a higher purpose (something both sides value and agree on).** So here's how we plan to move forward in a way that will uphold existing curricular foundations while thoughtfully integrating some of

the new approaches. Together, this will give students not only a solid command of math fundamentals, but also the creative-thinking abilities they need to tackle all kinds of real-world math challenges.

It's important to note that in some situations, such as crises, emergencies, or critical pivots, leaders may need to implement rapid, sweeping changes that don't preserve existing policies or procedures. Even in these cases, the Both/And approach remains valuable.

While the specific practices may change dramatically, leaders can still affirm and maintain core strengths such as team cohesion, organizational values, quality standards, and customer service reputation. This helps provide a sense of continuity and stability amidst significant upheaval, making the transition more manageable for team members.

THE MERGER MINEFIELD

Another significant change I've helped many clients navigate is understanding and adjusting to a merger or acquisition. Even when the strategic rationale for combining companies is sound, it can spark significant resistance if not approached and communicated properly.

Too often, companies take an Either/Or approach, communicating why the merger is the only logical choice while hyping all the utopian benefits everyone will soon enjoy. However, employees frequently resist because their sole focus is on the fear of losing their identity, their processes, and what made their original company successful in the first place.

There is a better way! Let's say Company A, an established manufacturing firm, is merging with Company B, an innovative tech startup. By using the Getting Unstuck model, leaders can minimize resistance and build genuine buy-in for the merger's greater purpose.

1. **Start by affirming the positive results of stability.** Company A has built a strong reputation over decades for quality craftsmanship, operational excellence, and a committed, tenured workforce. These are valuable strengths that cannot be discarded.

2. **Next, validate the negative results of change if it's overdone.** The merger understandably raises concerns about disrupting the well-oiled processes, client relationships, and cultural norms that have made Company A successful. And overdone change could jeopardize quality and customer loyalty.

3. **Then, explore the positive results of change.** AND Company B brings cutting-edge technologies, an entrepreneurial mindset, and a direct connection to emerging markets that will help the combined entity stay ahead of the curve and open new growth opportunities.

4. **Finally, discuss how leveraging the positive results of both change and stability can achieve a higher purpose.** So here's how we plan to preserve Company A's proven core strengths while injecting Company B's innovative capabilities so we can become the premier, built-to-last industry leader.

In any situation involving a major change—whether a curriculum overhaul, company merger, or strategic shift—people will not fully engage with the vision until two conditions are met. First, they must believe you understand and will preserve what they deeply value about the current state. Second, they need confidence that you grasp their specific fears about the changes and have a plan to mitigate the risks.

By utilizing the Getting Unstuck process, you provide a structured way to have those concerns genuinely heard and validated. This creates openness to then exploring the potential upsides of change. More than buy-in, it fosters authentic enthusiasm for how the new direction can achieve an even higher purpose that synthesizes everyone's core values.

THE REWARDS OF RISK

In Chapter 1, we explored some sobering research showing that nearly 70% of organizational change efforts fail to achieve their intended goals.[2] Throughout this book, we've examined the reasons behind this high failure rate and how to ensure your next change initiative succeeds.

However, before we conclude our time together, I want to emphasize that change should not be seen as something to fear or avoid. Quite the opposite. I want you to feel empowered and excited about leading change. The cliché is true: Change is the only constant in life and work. But that's wonderful news you should embrace!

A few years ago, I went through a personal development program where one exercise proved incredibly insightful. The instructor had us identify the three best decisions of our lives.

Although I'd never thought about this before, it didn't take me very long to come up with my list:

1. As a first-year university student, on a bit of a whim,
    I decided to travel to a new country and spend
    my summer working at a guest ranch rather than
    going home. This opened up my world in ways that
    ultimately redefined both my educational and career
    path.

2. I overcame cynicism and apprehension to accept
    a friend's offer to set me up on a blind date. This
    resulted in meeting, falling in love with, and marry-
    ing my best friend, Becky.

3. I decided to leave my successful business to run a
    homeless shelter. This forced me to "walk my talk"
    and live out the leadership principles I had taught
    for years, and it allowed me to tap into a better,
    stronger version of myself.

Examining this list, I realized all my life's best decisions stemmed from embracing change—letting go of the known, comfortable realities to lean into uncertainty and risk. It reaffirmed for me what I believe is a universal truth: We can only tap into our full potential and make a lasting impact by courageously embracing change and being open to life's unpredictable adventures.

My hope is this book has not only provided strategies for leading change more effectively, but has also inspired you to feel genuinely excited about the vital change leadership role you get to play. Here's to helping yourself, your team, and your organization become truly great!

Only a Person Who Risks Is Free

To laugh is to risk appearing the fool.

To weep is to risk being called sentimental.

To reach out to another is to risk involvement.

To expose feelings is to risk exposing your true self.

To place your ideas, your dreams before the crowd is to risk being called naive.

To love is to risk not being loved in return.

To live is to risk dying.

To hope is to risk despair,

and to try is to risk failure.

But risks must be taken because the greatest hazard in life is to risk nothing.

The person who risks nothing does nothing, has nothing, and becomes nothing.

They may avoid suffering and sorrow, but they simply cannot learn and feel and change and grow and love and live.

Chained by certitudes, they are a slave, they have forfeited their freedom.

Only the person who risks is truly free.

LEO F. BUSCAGLIA

FREE RESOURCE

To thank you for purchasing this playbook, I want to provide you with a free resource that will allow you to create a personal action plan around key concepts and big ideas.

Simply visit www.timarnold.ca/change or scan the QR code above to download the Personal Action Plan. This digital journal includes chapter summaries, tension maps, and assessment grids as well as space for you to create a plan you can immediately put into action.

WWW.TIMARNOLD.CA/CHANGE

NEXT STEPS

Scan the QR code to check out these enjoyable and effective ways to help your entire organization tap into successful change management:

Keynotes – One-hour presentations that motivate your audience to move beyond divisive and limiting Either/Or thinking and embrace the transformational power of Both/And leadership. Virtual and in-person options available.

Workshops – Insightful and engaging virtual and in-person programs that boost morale, develop leadership, and align teams to thrive.

Online Course – A self-directed, five-module course that will help you thrive in a world of complexity and polarization. Includes teaching videos, an editable workbook, and reflection activities.

VISIT WWW.TIMARNOLD.CA TO BOOK TIM FOR YOUR NEXT EVENT.

"As an event professional, I've literally seen thousands of speakers, and I can count on one hand the number of speakers who 1) have a unique perspective on a topic that will change the way your audience thinks and 2) can deliver it in a way that keeps audiences engaged. Tim Arnold is at the top of that list! You won't go wrong booking Tim for your next event."

– ANH NGUYEN

PRINCIPAL AND CO-FOUNDER, SPARK EVENT MANAGEMENT

REFERENCES

CHAPTER 1

1. Chip Heath and Dan Heath, *Decisive: How to Make Better Choices in Life and Work.* Crown Currency, 2013.

2. Harvard Business Review, John P. Kotter, W. Chan Kim, and Renee A. Mauborgne, *HBR's 10 Must Reads on Change Management*, Harvard Business Review Press, 2011.

CHAPTER 2

1. Amy Edmondson, *Right Kind of Wrong: The Science of Failing Well.* Atria Books, 2023.

2. Amy Edmondson, *Strategies for Learning from Failure.* Harvard Business Review, 2011.

3. David Cooperrider and Diana Whitney, *Appreciative Inquiry: A Positive Revolution in Change.* Berrett-Koehler Publishing Inc., 2005.

4. Greg McKeown, *Essentialism: The Disciplined Pursuit of Less.* Crown Currency, 2020.

5. Simon Sinek, *How Great Leaders Inspire Everyone to Take Action.* Penguin Books, 2011.

CHAPTER 3

1. John P. Kotter, *Leading Change*. Harvard Business Review Press, 1996.

2. Daniel Goleman, *Emotional Intelligence: Why It Can Matter More Than IQ*. Bantam Books, 1995.

3. Elisabeth Kübler-Ross, *On Death and Dying*. Macmillan Publishing Company, 1969.

CHAPTER 5

1. David Kolb, *Experiential Learning: Experience as the Source of Learning and Development (Vol. 1)*. Prentice-Hall, 1984.

2. Stephen Silver, "The story of the original iPhone, that nobody thought was possible." *Apple Insider*, June 29, 2018, https://appleinsider.com/articles/18/06/29/the-story-of-the-original-iphone-that-nobody-thought-was-possible

CHAPTER 6

1. Donald Miller, *Building a StoryBrand: Clarify Your Message So Your Customers Will Listen*. HarperCollins Leadership, 2017.

2. Colin Camerer, George Loewenstein, and Martin Weber, "The Curse of Knowledge in Economic Settings: An Experimental Analysis." *Journal of Political Economy (Vol. 97, Issue 5)*, 1989.

CHAPTER 7

1. Barry Johnson, *And: Making a Difference by Leveraging Polarity, Paradox or Dilemma, (Volume One: Foundations).* HRD Press, 2020.

2. Harvard Business Review, John P. Kotter, W. Chan Kim, and Renee A. Mauborgne, *HBR's 10 Must Reads on Change Management*, Harvard Business Review Press, 2011.

ABOUT THE AUTHOR

Tim Arnold has spent over two decades helping leaders manage complexity, increase resilience, and deliver results within organizations such as the United Nations, Compassion International, Royal Bank of Canada, Allstate Insurance, Toyota, and Siemens.

After running both a for-profit business and a homeless shelter, Tim leverages his real-world experience to help organizations pursue both profit and purpose. His work focuses on helping leaders unleash the superpower of Both/And thinking in an Either/Or world.

Beyond leadership and team development, Tim is an avid fisherman, world traveller, and really bad hockey player. His biggest accomplishments are being dad to Declan and Avryl and husband to Becky.

WWW.TIMARNOLD.CA

WWW.LEADERSFORLEADERS.CA